Love

"Easy to find, Hard to keep"

By:

Enrique Rodriguez

ISBN: 978-1-4269-4901-2 (sc)
ISBN: 978-1-4269-4902-9 (e)

Trafford rev. 11/12/2010

 www.trafford.com

North America & international
toll-free: 1 888 232 4444 (USA & Canada)
phone: 250 383 6864 ♦ fax: 812 355 4082

Also look for my poetry book
Coming very soon in early 2011.

"Lonely Road"

Introduction

I thought I was erratic, I thought I was an enigma, but the truth is relationships are very hard to maintain. I have found that many times in a relationship either the girl is happy and the guy is uncertain, or the other way around. The solution to a healthy and long relationship depends on the line of <u>communication</u>, and amount of love and support for each other.

Finding love was not a huge deal for me, I would just go on dates, experiment my personality with other girls. One thing I have also found out about girls is that they need to feel that love no matter what, whether they act like they don't need it, or keep saying that they are ok on how they are treated, trust me they are always searching for the one that will love them unconditionally. So anytime that you can express your love and affection to your companion, just do it, life will be easier for you and your love, and maybe the amount of cheating on one another would actually drop.

All of our relationships have been productive at first. As months past by, that fresh air subsides. Before we know it, once again it becomes a non-productive relationship. You see, no communication, sense of insecurity, and with your mind wondering off thinking about the uncertain, that creates a non-productive relationship.

Finding love is as easy as 1-2-3, you just need to go out more, know what you are looking for, and most of all don't be too shy, open up a little, and remember just a little, you do not want to look desperate. Finding love is pretty easy, its just trying to keep that love that is very hard and challenging.

Ivan and Carmen, I consider them as my family, they have been great and supportive on any relationship I have been on. Ivan and Carmen have been married for about 3 years now, they are so much in love with each other, I love the way you guys express your love for one and other. You guys are truly what relationships should be all about nothing but love is expressed. I love you both and never change anything about your personalities, you guys are wonderful in every way.

Special thanks to Roger and Vanessa more great friends of mine who I consider family. They have been together for about 11 years now, yes 11 and still going strong, that is very rare in this day and age to go that long without letting the relationship go sour. They are the pinnacle in the relationship world and how it is suppose to be like. I love you both keep on going strong in your love and affection for one another.

In this book you will see past experiences from my friends, parents, and strangers that have been with each other through the thick and thin. You will find out the truth about dating, about love, and things that are very helpful to creating that bond that creates that thing called love. Thank you to my closest friends, my family, and people that took their time to talk to me about their experiences in their relationships, thank you all.

CONTENTS

Love

"Easy to find, Hard to keep"

CHAPTER I

"Finding Love"

For some, finding love can be a walk in the park, for others, finding love is as easy as winning the lotto, actually that is the case for many of us. "Love", What is the your definition of love? Some say tender passion, some say devotion, dedication to one and other, you can have a different definition for that, that is probably why that word is offend used in a relationship.

Some are afraid of that word, others treat it as they say "like what-ever". Love can only have one meaning in a serious relationship, a very deep feeling that soothes your soul.

I was in a relationship for about 5 months with a great girl, she would use that word almost every moment in our relationship. I felt good about it, but I always have wondered what her definition of "Love" was. She would also let me know that she would love me for ever and ever, well, that was not the case, we had some differences and off we went into our own paths because she was not feeling the love anymore.

So it hurt at first, I loss a lot of sleep, could not eat, or even think properly, but I just don't get how a girl can use that word so many times in such a short amount of time then break up with someone.....I laugh about now, but I believe that there was something else that happened. I later found out that she actually found someone else, got married and has a beautiful little girl, I wished her the best in her life with her new family. I am not bitter about it at all, I am very happy for her and I am glad to see that pensive girl that I knew, she deserves the best.

Finding the one that you want to be with can be challenging, but just be yourself, you don't want to be with someone that criticizes your every move, every word, and things that you are passionate about. One thing to look for when searching for your soul mate is body language. Just pay attention to details on your date, that can tell you a lot about the person that you are with.

For the girls meeting a guy for the first time, don't be too shallow and give that guy a chance. I know that on many occasions I found that some of my female friends would think about what if.......what if I would of given him a chance? Maybe it's the fact that my friends where afraid of having their hearts broken once again. When we think about the past too much, sometimes that can really hurt us in the present and future, it makes it harder to find that special one. You must consider this, <u>Life is too short </u>to dwell on the past, if you really want a future you must live in the present and think about the future.

Finding Love, that is what makes life living for. Finding love can be very easy, but finding the right one for you can be very mentally grueling. You tend to give up a lot when you find love, but remember, be 100% sure of that relationship because if there is any doubt about it, then you must wait before you sky dive into this great thing called love.

Tom (37 years old) and Jessica (36 years old)

Tom: "I met Jessica at this fund raiser for my daughter's school. From the very moment we locked eyes, I just knew I had to say something before the opportunity would go away. The first time I had the opportunity to say something, this is what I said, "Hi my name is Tom Gordon, and I am feeling butterflies in my stomach". I could not believe what came out of my mouth, I was so embarrassed but at the same time it made Jessica smile from ear to ear. I would have never imagine that something as silly as "butterflies in my stomach" would have connected me with the one that I have been looking for.

Jessica: "Me and Tom met while helping our kids at this fundraiser thing, I remember Tom glancing at me and I was thinking what in the world is he looking at. After I glance at him I actually liked the way he looked and I liked his personality, he seemed like a great guy. So when we finally met face to face, Tom said something cute, that he had butterflies in his stomach, I thought that was so adorable. I could tell that he was very nervous when he was saying that, and yes that is all it took for our journey together to begin."

In talking with both Tom and Jessica, they both were very happy and excited to talk about how they met, because lets face it that was a cute way of breaking the ice. They are both very happy together and their kids get along very well. You see, its that easy to find the one that you are looking for, but you must make the best out of any opportunity that is presented to you. As far as Tom and Jessica goes, that is a relationship made in heaven in my opinion.

CHAPTER 2

"Dating"

Oh yes!, the dating scene, isn't it great!, going out on different dates, but can't seem to find the right one. Dating can be so nice and fun, When you find someone like that, keep going on dates with that person, find out as much information as you possibly can. Sometimes it takes a while to get to know someone, but its better to know them, then not to know them at all. Me personally, I have had great girlfriends, but my problem was I had too much going on in my life. Too many distractions, so my problem was not having my life organized, because lets face it, no one wants to be involved with someone that is disorganized.

I am not a bad guy at all, but because of my struggles at that time I was stressed out, and not satisfied with my life. That old saying of good guys finish last, well it seemed very true at that time. I felt that the good girls wanted the bad boys, and the bad girls wanted the good boys, kind of the opposite attraction. But what I have found out over the period of my life is the fact that you must have things in common with that person, listening to that person will also win you some good points as well.

No one wants to be put in a situation where you are in a relationship for months and months just to teach the other person on how to be in a serious relationship. I have been in some of those and let me tell you that it is not a pleasant feeling. Dating can also be very intriguing, I think most of us have some nice and weird date stories.

Example 1: Like when the other person is too comfortable with you and acts like you have been dating for years.

Example 2: How about that person that right away gets into your personal problems and dislikes.

Finally 3: And the best for last, how about that person that takes calls or Texting while having a nice dinner or conversation.

Now when ever that happens, you should be smart enough to know, that is how its going to be in that relationship, Electronics will rule that great connection.

Have you ever been giving a fake phone number? Well many people have experience that, but do you know why you have received a bad phone number?......well I will tell you, I know for a fact that if a date is going to be successful all parts of social connections must align correctly. You might have been giving a bad phone number because of either, the communication level was not on the same level, 2, the expectations were not met for the other person, 3, you revealed a little too much for the other person to handle, or 4, you guys probably have totally different taste on life and other things. Remember don't get discourage, keep looking, take it as a stepping stone to the next date. I know that a lot of people get tired of dating, and many just relinquish dating, just don't give up, keep looking, there is always someone waiting for their soul mate and sometimes they are closer than you actually think.

So how do we deal with a first date, well, be yourself, you don't have to hype up yourself or make up stories so your date will actually like you. If any, you will probably intimidate your date, and that will create a very non-productive conversation. Consider this, once you lie, even though its not a big deal, it actually becomes a trust issue. The reason it would become a trust issue is the simple fact that it becomes a pattern, you start to lie on little things that later become a bigger situation.

I actually met these two people at sea port village in downtown san diego and they were actually on a first date! Wow! What a coincidence, I was working on this exact project, well this is what they were saying about each other.

Michelle (32 years old) and Steve (31 years old)'s first Date.

Michelle: "Hello my name is Michelle, and yes I am on my first date with Steven. It is going well, We have a good connection with one another, he is very easy going and he makes me laugh, that is a big plus for me. The last date I was on was about one month ago, so my friends egged me on for this date. But like I said, so far everything is good so I must wait and see what happens."

Me: "So, on the scale from 1 to 10, what do you think so far?."
(Remember they are separated at this time)

Michelle: "I would give him about an 8 for now."

Steven: "Was up man, yup this is our first date, and its going ok for now. So far she has talked about her past troubles and has talked about her ex boyfriend about 3 times now, that is the only thing that would bring this date to an end. She is a good girl, but I need stability in my relationship, and she should not be talking about her past troubles a lot and about her ex, it just does not sit well with me."

Me: "on the scale from 1 to 10, what do you think so far?."

Steven: "don't tell her this, but…….for now its about a 2."

I was as surprised as many of you to hear this from Steve. But they are on their first date, so I guess you can give him the benefit of a doubt. If there was anything to learn from that date, it was that never ever talk about your troubles and ex on the first date, that is a recipe for disaster. Give the date a chance to grow, because you never know if he/she is the one.

Chapter 3

"Great Times"

You get to the fun part of the relationship, the great times. You and your partner are head over heels for each other, you guys go out a lot, you can't stop thinking of one another, and your friends and family are always asking when do we get to meet this person that is making you look silly. When you get to this point, you tend to think about kids, marriage, and a life time of happiness.

Make sure not to be too spontaneous, relax, take a deep breath, because I found out the hard way what the ramifications would be when you act out on pure passion and not true love. I know that it feels great, the feeling that soothes your soul, and makes you feel alive. We all get lost in love from time to time, that is perfectly normal, just have fun with the one that you are with, keeps things fresh and outgoing.

Tom: "We are having a great time together, we go out and do a lot of family things. She listens very well, so our communication is excellent."

Jessica: "We have many great times together, Tom is a wonderful man, and our kids love hanging out with each other. We take many family trips and enjoy each other's company. Since the first time we have met we have had about 90% great times, 5% relaxing time, and 5% struggles. But overall our relationship is still in that Great times as you say."

Tom and Jessica are the type of role models that we crucially need to be emulating in our relationship. Meeting them was a blessing in the sky, they are great human beings and I was honored to have talked with them.

Consider this, like I tell my friends, dealing with a difficult break-up for every person there is one waiting to spend their rest of their life with you. Never relinquish, never loose hope, stay the way you are, what makes you, you. Great times can last a lifetime, so this stage can never go away, that is if you loose that will and passion for your partner. If you ever need an inspiration because your relationship is on the edge, just simple look back to how that relationship started, be that pensive person you were when you first met. If it was meant to be, everything will fall in place.

The mother of my Son, Yolanda, when I met her she showed me a personality that I have never ever seen before. She was very outgoing, very nice with me, super friendly with me. I actually thought that we had a very bright future, and that relationship looked very promising. But boy was I wrong, ladies please do not pretend to be nice, do not pretend that you have a wonderful heart if you really don't. I treated her like gold, I would take her out for lunch, dinner, and even bring her flowers, but something about her was just not right. You see, we worked together at that time, our co-workers would warn me about her, but a couple of things that had me thinking about going out with her was the fact that her friends and own family warm be about her......man I should of taken their advice, now I am paying child support and I have had 0% visitation with my son. Her problem, from what one of her closest friends told me, was the fact that once the fun was over, she would shut down.

This is what happens a lot in relationships, we all look for more fun, and less stress. It would be nice to have that luxury, but this is life, we are all going to struggle in relationships. My very good friends Roger and Vanessa have had their share of struggles, they have some differences, but they compromise with each other, and that is why they have been together for over 11 years now and its still going stronger than ever.

If great times is not present in a relationship or it suddenly vanishes, you better think long and hard whether or not this relationship is worth salvaging. Remember, If you want it to work, you must put in work, relationships are suppose to be very difficult, if it is too easy, then something is not right and just talk about it to your love one.

We all dread having a mediocre relationship, so we tend to be very picky with choosing our partner. But when you are having great times together, it really becomes a non factor in choosing a person with the same qualities as you.

CHAPTER 4

"The Transformation"

This is the part of the relationship that we don't like to go thru. Everything has changed, and this relationship has taken a 360 degree turn. What has happened?, How did we get to this point?, well it can be many things that has caused this to happen. Maybe one or the both of you are second guessing each other. Maybe you feel like you don't want to change, or simple, the both of you are afraid of commitment. But one thing you must understand, if that person makes you feel great, alive, and has the possibility of a long-term deal with you, talk it out and see where you both stand, maybe its just as simple as a little communication to help you guys through this transformation.

We all tend to feel things, gut feelings, and if you see your girlfriend, or boyfriend looking kind of gloomy, again, communication will be the most essential tool both of you would need to make it through this gloomy time. Lack of communication, trust, and love will diffidently lead to the demise of that relationship.

The transformation stage isn't all bad, sometimes it can lead up to a better and more rewarding situation. For example, lets just say that this relationship has been all but soothing, it has caused stressed, mental pain, and even bad habits. In the transformation stage it will either build the relationship stronger, by learning from your mistakes and fixing it right away or just completely eradicate the love and passion that was once there.

I was walking along the shores of imperial beach when I saw this couple holding hands and giving kisses to one another. Well, I am writing a book about love so I thought I should see if they can share some incite on their experience with love.

Jorge (27 years old) and Christina (29 years old)

Jorge: "My name is Jorge, I am from San Diego. I have been with Christina for about 5 months now. We met at her brother's birthday party, it was the very first time that I have met her in person, and I just fell for her hard. She is a great girl, with a very joyful attitude, and a love for life. Her heart is unmatched, and that is why she absolutely stole my heart."

Me: "You guys seem very happy together and seem to have so much love for each other."

Jorge: "Oh yes!, she is the best thing that has ever happened to me, I would do anything for my Christina."

Me: "So if there was anything negative in this relationship what do you think that would be?."

Jorge: "Are you kidding me (jokingly laughing), so far there is nothing that I see that would even cross my mind about being negative, Between me and you…..I'm in love."

Me: "This conversation will be about "The Transformation", have you experienced that in the relationship at this time?."

Jorge: "Transformation?? (Smiling) nope, nothing like that, I think that if we do go through that, we will just have to adapt to it."

Christina: "Hi my name is Christina, born and raised in San Diego, I met Jorge at my brother's birthday party about 5 months ago, he is a great guy and really caters to my needs."

Me: "So, in the 5 months of being together, what are your deepest thoughts good or concerns about Jorge?."

Christina: "Well…….everything has been great, pretty much perfect at this point. I love the way he looks at me, I love the way he talks with me, but most of all, I love the way he is honest with me, I am very big on truthfulness."

Me: "you just said that trust is very crucial to you, but besides trust, what other quality makes you feel head over heels for him?".

Christina: "He is a very charming guy, very good hearted, and genuinely cares about me and this relationship."

Me: "on a scale from 1 to 10, how would you rate this relationship at this point?."

Christina: "a 10! I love him and he loves me, this is perfect, I would not ask for anyone else."

Wow, I keep bumping into these excellent couples, Jorge and Christina are really in love. As I was talking with each of them, they showed a lot of passion when they described their relationship. I wish them the best of luck, and I know as long as the Transformation don't get to them, they are going to be fine.

Things change, they always do, that is relevant in life, but what makes life living is adapting, moving forward and not backwards. Just remember, relax, take a step back and realize what you must do to keep your relationship in tack.

Being in this stage, is a tough and rough situation to be in for the both of you, don't worry too much, all of us go through this at one point in our relationships. Remember, just be yourself, and look back to what made this relationship great.

CHAPTER 5

"Fixing the Problem"

Now we try and conquer the problem that is making the relationship decrease in passion. Weather its about something small or something that would make you second guess the relationship, there are always a way to fixing the problem no matter what. I can recall a friend of mine Oscar. Oscar married his high school sweetheart, they have 2 kids together and have been very much in love.

Well, one day Oscar asked me, "What do you think my life would be like, without the loves in my life". That sounded very peculiar to me, so I redirected the question back to him, and the look on his face was pure sadness, he responded, "I would be a miserable man", " I thank god for having them in my life everyday".

Problems are very relevant in relationships, no matter what age, culture, or the amount of time together. The important thing to remember is communication, but try to converse in a matter where you respect the other person's opinions, feelings and not in a sarcastic way. Little things like that can create a big problem, at this point you want to avoid anything big, because you know that the relationship is on the verge of failure, you do not want it to end after all that you have been through. Remember, just relax, and reminisce on how you met, and keep in mind that problems all always going to be around in relationships, your are not the only one that has them, we all go through that every time, just don't worsen the situation, make things right with the one that you love.

Always think back on what got you both together in the first place. Sometimes all it takes is a little spark to get the passion going again, be creative, think of new and exciting ways to please your love one, weather in the bed, or as simple as a nice night out with a romantic theme, or the always traditional walk in the park.

Roger and Vanessa have 2 kids together, Roger has 1 kid from a previous relationship. They are not married but have been together for about 11 years and counting. It is amazing that after all of those years they are still very much in love. One day I have asked, "How do you guys do it?", Vanessa simply Smiled and said jokingly "Well he gets abused when he does not listen!", Roger just laughs and goes along with that answer. It is that simple, just keeping an honest and open mind with one another, they realized that keeping a pensive and loquacious attitude with one and other keeps the relationship up to beat and never a dull moment with those two, they have such a positive attitude, they listen to one other, and even after 11 years together, they still have the same attitude as when the first time they got together. But like other relationships, they have had their share of problems, but they work through that and at the end they always end up compromising with each other.

Remember, Communication is the key to a successful relationship, whether married or not, I have seen so many infidelities, so many divorces, and so many broken down souls that are never the same when they start dating again. Remember, Fixing the problems are communications, love and trust.

I bump into this girl sitting along at Iris park. She looked like she was sad and just thinking way too much. So asked if I would be able to ask some questions for a research I was doing. She hesitated for a moment but then agreed to it. Now as I was getting ready to start, this guy gets there and asked who was I. I explained to him I was doing a research on couples, and I asked if he was her boyfriend or husband. He said boyfriend, So I asked him about joining me in a research project, he thought I was joking but once he saw I was serious, he reluctantly agreed.

Jose (23 years old) and Jennifer (20 years old)

Me: "So I see that you guys are having some problems, Jose, in your opinion, what do you think is causing this?

Jose: "Well besides, her going out a lot with her friends, and we don't really see each other as much".

Jennifer: "Its not like we are married, I can go out with my friends and have a social life!"

Jose: "yes that's fine, but about us, what about this relationship?", Do you still want to be with me?"

Jennifer: "I have mixed emotions, I want to be with you but you must also give me my space".

Me: "Now if I can just ask both of you something, and Jennifer I will ask you first, it seems to me that Jose is committed to this relationship, what is stopping you from giving more time to Jose?".

Jennifer: "well, I guess we are growing apart, I really don't know at this time, all I know is that I must have time with my friends at this point"(Tears running down her cheek).

At this time Jose told me that they needed time to their selves to work out things, I thanked them for giving me the time to ask some questions in these rough times that they are having.

What did we see in this very brief interview?, well I know that we see a problem that is just moments away from a break up. I was observing both of them, and in my opinion Jose was showing much more interest in the relationship than Jennifer was. I think that in order to fix that problem, would be two different things that would have to happen, 1 would be that Jose must back off a bit and give Jennifer the time she needs to figure out what she really wants, or 2, would be to let go of the relationship that is heading over the edge very quickly. I would not recommend breaking up at first, I would suggest, giving the relationship a chance, talk it out, and give the other person what he/she wants.

Let them think about what they really want, you just be understanding, and supportive in any way possible and just show that person that you still care about them.

Remember, the crucial key factors in fixing a relationship would be, Communications, love and understanding. If the other person wishing not go on with the relationship, then it was just not meant to be. Its not the end of the world, but like I said just follow those rules and if it was meant to be, everything will work out somehow and someway.

CHAPTER 6

"The Way It Was"

Many couples panic, they always think that the relationship is taking a turn for the worst. Many ask themselves how did we get to this point?, I want things the way they us to be, but how can I make it that way once again?.

We all see these reality shows that involved husband and wife, or girlfriend and boyfriend. Most of them end up breaking up, most of them end up not even communicating with one and other. That is how this is, we love how it use to be, because those times were fun, exciting, and rather new to us. That is exactly what we look for, a new excitement in our lives.

Our minds can play tricks on us, it makes us wonder, makes us sad, even makes us question the future, but the fact of the matter is, you have to live in the present, learn from the past, in order to control your future.

Samething goes in a relationship, we all learn from our past mistakes. If you look back, what do you think would be the worst habit you had?. If you were to correct that habit today, what do you think your relationship would be like?. One person in particular did just that, he told me that he has had a very bad habit, a habit that would ultimately lead to the break up with his girlfriend. Jesse, a 29 year old guy I have met playing basketball for many years. He told me that his biggest habit would be that, he simply shuts down after about 3 months of dating, he does not give the relationship any chance whats so ever after the 3 months. So I asked him, "Why do you think you go through the same motion every time in your relationships?", and he said, "I just get bored for some reason, like if I need to feel excitement after those months have passed by". That was a very true statement, well one of them, the other thing I believe was a problem for him was the fact that he was afraid of commitment, and responsibility, at the time that he chooses to shut down is the time that he feels responsibilities coming on.

If you really want to get back to the way it was, be yourself again, don't be afraid of commitement, and take on the responsibilities that presents it self to you. When you start taking those things seriously, guess what, it makes you grow into a mature and intelligent person, not only Is it going to help your relationship out, its going to teach you important things that will help you live a great life.

I went back to imperial beach, I was in search for a couple that has been through their ups and downs in their relationship. But let me tell you, it was not easy, people were in a different mood at that time, but after about 1 hour and a half of searching I found an older couple in their 40's, I am pretty sure that they have been through rough times at some point in their relationship.

Mike (44 years old) and Debra (42 years old)

Me: "How long have you been with Debra?".

Mike: "I have been with Debra for about 21 years now and have been married for about 17 years".

Me: "Oh that is great, so how did you both meet?".

Mike: "Well, we met in college at SDSU, she was studying to be an English proffesor, and I was studying architecture.

Me: "How do you as a couple survive in these rough times?."

Mike: "Let me tell you, it is not easy sometimes, but the good thing is the fact that we get along so well and compromise with each other's needs, we help one and other, and we have become a great team together."

Me: "Can you recall a time when you were asking yourself, I wish things can get back to the way it was?."

Mike: "I can recall one time out of our 21 year relationship, it was about 5 to 6 years ago, we were having problems with bills, we have just had our 3rd kid together and things were just not going well as they use to, I was actually asking myself that question many times for months and months, but I never relinquished and thank god Debra never did either." "We got through it with a lot of love and understanding, and the will to stay together because we knew that we would be miserable without one and other, we paid our bills, a little late but paid off, and now we are doing great, we have learned from our mistakes and we are more in love than ever."

Debra: "Hello, my name is Debra, I met Mike in college, and right away we clicked."

Me: "What was your first impression when you met Mike?."

Debra: "He was and is a very handsome man, I loved the way he would talk to me with complete respect." "Just with that alone was enough to go out with him with no hesitation at all."

Me: "Did you ever go through a stage when you were asking yourself, How can I get things the way they were?."

Debra: "well, there was a time we were struggle ling with bills and we were having our 3rd child, but I really knew that we would eventually get out of it, just for the simple fact that we work together to overcome adversity at all times."

Me: "So did you ever think at that time, that this relationship would finally fail?."

Debra: "Never!, when I married Michael I made an oath to be with my husband through the thick and thin no matter what ramifications comes to us." " I love him with all of my heart, and he loves me because he shows me every time we are together."

I thank them both for the time and opportunity in speaking with me and It was time to go home. It was amazing, these two were head over heels for each other, even after all of this time they love each other unconditionally. You see, they worked together to make things right, that is the traditional way of doing it, because as we all should know is that one punch may not inflict a lot of damage, but when you punch with 2 fist, it can be a very effective blow.

So, in making things the way they were, you must compromise with each other, have faith in each other, respect one and other, and work as a team, because if one person wants to conquer the problems by themselves, that relationship will soon be over.

CHAPTER 7

"My Past Relationships"

In order to achieve the triumph of a great relationship, you must look back and reflect on your past relationships. I always believed that the reason why there are break-ups, is so that we learn from the mistakes made in that or those relationships.

In my observations in my past relationships, I can recall being very timid and casual with my girlfriend at that time. At first I would be very spontaneous, I did that so I can impress the girl, it worked, I would always show my girlfriend a good time. You must be fun, outgoing, and have good communication skills with your partner. That will always keep your relationship fresh and upbeat.

Ask yourself, what was the real reason why your past relationships were not successful?, once you come to realize why that relationship or relationships did not work, you can actually make things much more easier by eliminating all of the bad habits you once had, and apply new and better habits.

What are good habits?

1.) Being funny and ability to loosen up your partner.

2.) The ability to have a pleasant conversation.

3.) Listening to your partner.

4.) going out to romantic places from time to time.

5.) And one of the most important habits to have is, the habit to do what ever it takes to make your partner happy.

If you have some of those qualities you should be fine, lets just hope that the person you are seeing have some of those qualities as well, because remember, one person can not hold a relationship together forever, it always fails that way. In order for it to function, both of you must do things as a team, because whether your married or not, being in a relationship means doing pretty much everything together as one.

I went to the H St. shopping mall in Chula Vista, there I met with a couple who have been together for 6 years, they are not married and have no kids together, this should be an intriguing conversation.

Miguel (29 years old) and Stephanie (29 years old)

Miguel: "I met Stephanie here at this mall, we worked together at Sears." "She was a cashier, and I was a shift manager."

Me: "so, what was your first impression of Stephanie?."

Miguel: "She is very cool girl, she is outgoing and very talkative, I love that in a girl."

Me: "so the both of you have been together for 6 years." "Does Stephanie ever ask about marriage?," "and if so what do u think of that?."

Miguel: "Stephanie always ask about marriage, and I always say that we must let it fall into place." "But to tell you the truth, I am going to surprise her with a marriage proposal next week, because next week will officially be our 6 year anniversary." "Don't let her know."(Smiling)

Me: "Thank you for giving me the time to ask a few questions".

Stephanie: "You're welcome".

Me: "So let me start by asking you, When you first went out on your first date with Miguel, what was you first impression?".

Stephanie: "I actually thought that he was a little player as they say, but I was wrong, he is a wonderful man with a warm heart".

Me: "What would be the biggest asset to you about Miguel?".

Stephanie: "Miguel has been with me through the thick and thin, (Tearing up) Sorry getting a little emotional".

Me: "Its ok take your time, he seems like a very cool and collective guy".

Stephanie: "Yes he really is, I love the way he listens to me, and the way he surprises me from time to time with flowers or gifts".

Me: "What would be the ultimate payoff in this relationship?".

Stephanie: "Marriage, and two kids, a boy and a girl".

Me: "That is a very nice payoff, well I wish you both the best of luck and thank you both for taking the time to talk with me".

Stephanie: "Thank you for your time as well and take care of yourself, and we want a copy(Laughing)".

I hugged them both and was on my way.

I tried to bring up the past relationships but they both wished not to talk about them because they respect each other too much. From the body language they both gave me at that time when I asked them about their past relationships, I could tell that their experiences must have been hurtful or not meaningful at all. But never the less they are great together, and the proposal coming up could not come at a better time, I am really excited for what is about to happen in that relationship, it could not happen to a better couple and it is 6 years in the making.

So when it comes to past relationships, remember, everything happens for a reason, the break-ups, the fighting, and the disagreements. Determine whether or not the relationship is worth saving?, if so, then work things out. The only way you can become a better person in your new relationship, is by learning from the past.

CHAPTER 8

"Making It Work"

Now we get to the real work stage of the relationship. How do we make it work?, how do I compromise without jeopardizing my relationship?, we can ask ourselves those questions over and over again, but the truth of the matter is, if you put in no effort what so ever to at least try to make it work, then you might as well start looking elsewhere for love.

Trying to make it work in a situation were there is obviously some dissention, and less communication involved in the rapidly decreasing relationship, you must keep your cool and talk it out, either that spark is still there and you must explore what has happened in that relationship.

Now, sadly there are a lot of relationships that involve physical abuse, and there are a lot of people that would not condone that action 100%, including yours truly. Years and years ago, I had this friend. He and his girlfriend at that time were spending everyday and every night together, they were truly an item. Well, one day I slept over on the couch, it was about 2am, and I can hear arguing and a little bit of crying, next thing you know the crying gets a little louder and the girl says "you hit me in the eye!"(crying). From what I was listening to, it looks like my friend at that time threw her cell phone to her and hit her by her eye. I was pretending to be asleep when they came out of the room, my friend told his girlfriend to get all of her stuff and that he did not want to see her ever again. Well, guess what, one week later they went out to eat and starting to hang out again, I have been studying psychology for years now, I have studied the theories of Sigmund Freud, one of the founders of psychology, and Wilhelm Wundt who opened the first psychology lab in Leipzig, Germany. But it still confuses the heck out of me, when a girl keeps going out with an abusive guy. I would think that its probably about emotional attachment, and/or physical attachment. Whatever it is, girls, there are plenty of men ready to show real love, its not the end of the world.

Making the relationship work can be very tough, and sometimes exhaust you. But no matter what, always ask yourself, "Do I really want this to work?" of course you do, that is the person that you love, the person that you possibly have kids with, and the person that you probably are married to. Many people don't understand what marriage is really all about, like this couple that you are about to meet. I met this couple at the Horton Plaza in downtown San Diego, They have been married for about 1 year now and they were coming across as teens in a marriage situation. Well, they sure turned the tables on me!.

Melissa (27 years old) and Joshua (28 years old)

Me: "Hi Melissa how are you today?".

Melissa: "Good thank you, how are you?".

Me: "Good thanks, so lets get this started, so how did you and Joshua meet?".

Melissa: "We use to work together at Mervyn's, I was a cashier and he was in stocking, he came over and would talk with me every chance he would have, at first I did not think of him very much, but after about 3 months of talking and talking, I was single and he was single so we decided to hook up, and we have been together ever since".

Me: "Very nice, how long were you two dating till he popped the question?.

Melissa: We were dating for about 5 months only, and then he propose to me".

Me: "So how is the married life?, and what is the best part of the married life?".

Melissa: "The married life is great, I love everything about it". I would say the best part about being married is...........the open marriage part!"(Giggle ling).

Me: "Wow that came out of no where(Laughing)". "Well, that is perfectly fine and I know that you guys will last a very long time.

Joshua: "Was up guy".

Me: "Nice to meet you, so how is the married life treating you?".

Joshua: "Its all good, and considering that we have an open marriage!(laughing)".

Me: "Oh you don't say, do any of you two ever wonder or get jealous at all?".

Joshua: "No, not at all, it is a lot of fun, if you ever get married you should have an open marriage as well, so you can see how much fun it really is".

Me: "Yes I will keep that in mind(Smiling), Well I guess I already know what the best quality is in this marriage, so, before the openness of this marriage, what would be the main thing that wanted you to get married to Melissa?".

Joshua: "Her smile, she has a smile that would make me fall to my knees, and her personality, a huge plus, we just got along with each other very well and felt really comfortable every time we hung out together".

Me: "Thank you and your wife for the time to talk to me, you both are looking very happy with each other and hope that nothing but happiness comes along for the both of you".

Joshua and Melissa: "Thank you!(Shaking my hand)".

So off I went thinking, holly smokes, that was a very intriguing couple!. We all must think correctly with an open mind, just like they did, well if you must add a little something to the marriage to spice things up, just be prepared for the ramifications that awaits you. Having an open marriage can be fun, but it can be very stressful in a way. So if you want things the way it was, talk with your love one, go back to basics, as corny as that sounds it works, just try it out.

CHAPTER 9

"Understanding Relationships"

Are you still scratching your head?, still wondering why nothing is working. Are you understanding your partner of his/her needs?. We all wonder these things, but the ones that do something about it are the ones who actually succeed. Remember that communications is a huge tool you will need to successfully accomplish a relationship you have been desperately searching for.

3 main rules to having a successful relationship.

1) Devotion

2) Love

3) Understanding

Devotion, when you are wiling to give your time and effort to making a relationship work, that is what real Devotion is all about.

Love, that is the single most important thing to have, if you are looking to have a long and happy marriage some day.

Understanding, this is another important key element to having a successful relationship, in order to please your partner, you must first understand your partner.

Understanding your partner will take time to achieve, none of us are capable of understanding one and other right away. Some of us will actually take up to one year to maybe 3-4 years to get your partner. Its ok, it's a normal situation, just show your partner a good time and everything else will fall into place.

I went on a little trip to the beach, mission beach to be exact. I saw many couples and many of them turned me down for an interview, but I did manage to get an interview with a couple, but I had to buy them a drink or two. This couple opened up very well and gave it to me straight.

Justin (26 years old) and Megan (26 years old)

Me: "So Justin, How did you meet Megan?".

Justin: "we met at my friend's house party about 4 years ago".

Me: "What attracted you to her?".

Justin: "She has a very nice body, and she looked nice and innocent, so I asked her if she wanted to dance, and after that we hooked up".

Me: "so after 4 years of being together, how do you feel about her now?".

Justin: "I love her, we do everything together, we have a lot of fun, we go out to the clubs, we go out on road trips, we get along very well".

Me: "Nice to meet you Megan, I am only going to ask a few questions about you and Justin".

Megan: "Sure, ask away"(Smiling).

Me: "What was your first impression about Justin?".

Megan: "Well, lets see, he had a beautiful smile, and the way he talked to me made him look like a very sweet guy, so I would say that the first impression was very good".

Me: "In any moment of the relationship, did you both compromise with each other to make something work?, if so then give me an example".

Megan: "Yes, quite a few actually, but this one time that I will always remember was, I wanted to go out with Justin for a romantic night out, but he had plans with his guy friends, well, he cancelled with no hesitation at all with his buddies and we had a night to remember, and that was when I knew that we were meant for each other".

Me: "Are there any things that you or Justin can work on to make things easier on the relationship?".

Megan: "Yes, I think we both can be a little more understanding of things, although we get along very well, it would be perfect if we compromise with each other much more".

Me: "So, What is next?".

Megan: "Marriage of course".

I thanked them both and they both hugged me and actually told me that I helped them understand their true feelings for each other and have a very clear perspective about their relationship. They are a great couple, and deserve nothing but the best things to happen in their relationship.

Understanding each other is an essential part of making the relationship last. Listen to each other, pay attention to one and other, take notes if you really have too, whatever it takes to understand the relationship and where it is heading. Remember that it takes work to get the relationship that you really want, a lot of communicating, compromising, love and trust, if you add that to your relationship, you should do just fine.

CHAPTER 10

"Lifetime Of Love"

Well for all of my readers, the end is near. For this final chapter I Went on a search to find 2 elderly couple that have been together for a very long time. Well, I was working as an optician, and I had this couple that looked so happy with each other and looked like they knew each other very well. So I asked them if I could take just a few minutes of their time and they gladly agreed, well, sit back, relax and check out what real love is all about, in what I appropriately call "Lifetime Of Love".

Peter (89 years old) and Susan (87 years old)

Me: "Thank you both very much for taking this opportunity to answer my questions, this is an absolute honor".

Peter and Susan: "Thank you".

Me: "So first I will be talking with Mrs. Williams one on one and then with you Mr. Williams if that is ok with you sir?".

Peter: "Yes, absolutely".

Me: "Ok, so when was the very first time you laid eyes on Peter?".

Susan: "Well actually, we went to the same high school together, he invited me to the under the stars dance, I said yes and our journey began".

Me: "Other than the dance, where was another place that the both of you went on a date?".

Susan: "back then, long time ago(Laughing), the county fair were very popular, and he took me there the next day after the dance, I can still remember all of the wonderful rides, and the wonderful times we had that night, it was such a glorious day for me, and that was the day were I fell in love with Peter".

Me: "In the new Generation, couples tend to break-up when times get really rough, how did you deal with the rough times and stayed together through the thick and thin?".

Susan: "Well, Love is a big and important feeling to have for one and other, and I think that the reason for all of the divorces and break-ups is specifically about love".

Me: "After all of this time of being with Peter, how would you define true love?".

Susan: "Well lets see, What true love means for me is…..having a very strong feeling for the other person, we would do whatever it would take to make each other happy, and we would stand behind one and other through our difficult times, and love is a very wonderful feeling, and love is something that will never die".

Me: "Thank you very much for your outlook on love, and hope nothing but wonderful things for you and your husband".

Susan: "Thank you for taking your time to talk with me".

Now it was time to get the scoop from Mr. Williams and see what he has gone through in this fairy tail relationship.

Me: "Ok, let me get started with my questions"……

Peter: "Yes please, because I don't have much time if you know what I mean"(Laughing).

Me: "Yes sir(Laughing), ok, so what attracted you to Susan?".

Peter: "My Sweetheart, yes, I was hanging out with the guys, and I saw her passing by in the hall ways, I glanced at her and I could not keep my eyes off of her, I invited Susan to the school dance with the theme name "Under the stars", and I right away knew that I had to make her my girl".

Me: "So how do you both get through the hard times?".

Peter: "Lets just say this, do whatever your wife tells you to do(Laughing), it will be easier for you and especially for your love one, and I am being honest about that, there is no other way, you must please your wife or girlfriend as much as you can, just keep her happy".

Me: "So how was it in the beginning of the relationship?".

Peter: "It was very good, we got along with each other very well, and we had a lot of fun together and we still do, we would listen to the radio together, we would go after school to the near café and have our soda pops together, and our friends all knew each other, lets just say that we had a wonderful time in the beginning".

Me: "What does true love mean to you?".

Peter: "It can mean many things, but to me it means having a very deep passionate feeling for the person that you love, wiling to do what ever it takes to make that person happy".

Me: "If you had only one wish, what would that be?".

As I asked that question, Mr. Williams started to have a little twinkle, as his eyes started to water up and this is exactly what he said.

Peter: "For this love never to end".

I hugged him and told him that I wish that their were more gentlemen just like him, and I was truly honored to have spoken with each of them on the subject matter of love.

Sometimes love can mean many things as Mr. Williams had said to me, but in reality, it is what you are wiling to do and sacrifice for that person that really defines love. Always remember, even if you cannot make a relationship work, always look back to the mistakes that you made and correct them, because there is always that one person waiting to spend the rest of their life with you, but you must be out in the open in order to find that special one. Just like Mr. and Mrs. Williams even the most corny things in life, can create a lifetime of love.

Extended Questions
Tom and Jessica

Me: "If you were to sum up your first impression of Jessica, what would that one word be?".

Tom: "Gorgeous!"

Me: "can you recall a time where the both of you clashed on an issue or opinion that both of you were standing by strong on?".

Tom: "Yes, there was this one time where I wanted a certain color in our restroom, she wanted to make it girly, and I wanted to make it not girly"

Me: "So how did you both agree on that decision? And what happened after that little disagreement?".

Tom: "We agreed on making it nice and modern, to the point where it was not girly and not that manly either, it actually gave us a nice perspective on our relationship, after getting through that we felt we can get through many other disagreements as well".

Me: "If you were to sum up your first impression of Tom, what word would you use to describe that impression?".

Jessica: "cute!".

Me: "Where did you guys go on your first date?".

Jessica: "Tom Took me to this very nice Italian restaurant in downtown, he was very handsome, very charming, and very romantic, it was a very perfect first date!".

Me: "Give me an example of a time where you both struggled to understand each other?".

Jessica: "There was this time where he was still hanging out with his buddies a lot, and I felt like that spark was going away, but the fact of the matter was that he is very loyal to his friends and he has shown me that he is very loyal to me and my kids, so he felt bad and started to hang out with me more and really proved that his love for me and my kids is 100% real".

Me: "Where would you want this relationship to be in about 5 years from now?".

Jessica: "Of course married, and maybe one more kid with Tom, I think that would the ultimate dream for me".

Michelle and Steven's First Date

Me: "Despite this being your first date with Steven, can you see yourself with Steven in a long term relationship?".

Michelle: "I really would like to say yes, but he has not really shown too much interest in me yet, but I think we can both make this work if he really wants to".

Me: "In your gut feeling, do you think Steven has what it takes to please you?".

Michelle: "I think he is funny, he kind of has a dry sense of humor, but I think he would have what it takes to make me happy, he just has to start showing a little more interest in me".

Me: "So Steven, what was your first impression of Michelle?".

Steven: "I looked at her and said dam, she is cute".

Me: "If she would have not been talking about her ex, past, and current problems, what would be your impression of her up to this moment?".

Steven: "I think that we would have been getting along much better, I will give this girl one more chance to make this a good date, but she needs to stop talking about all of her personal issues, this is a first date".

Me: "If she stops talking about all of those things that annoy you, do you think that this relationship can be a long term deal?".

Steven: "that would be a big MAYBE, it all depends on our likes and dislikes, and do we really have that passion for one and other".

Jorge and Christina

Me: "When was the last time you both had arguments, and how did you both get through it?

Jorge: "about a month ago or so, we got into an argument about something small, not a big deal at all, it was an argument about her mother, she did not want to go and visit her mother at that time, I did not know the reason why, so I instigated the situation and we got into a very silly argument about it, and it all get fixed after she explained that they were not seeing eye to eye on that day because of some words that were said".

Me: "What was your first impression on meeting Christina's parents?".

Jorge: "They were so hospitable towards me, and treated me like her husband, so my impression I guess you can say was very good!".

Me: "So how do you both get through the rough times together?".

Christina: "we talk things out every time when either Jorge or I see one and other looking sad and serious, communication has been a huge part of our relationship working the right way day in and day out".

Me: "what is the most important thing that really attracted you to Jorge, the one thing that made you want to be with him?".

Christina: "I am not the type that cares very much about the exterior appearance, it's the inside of Jorge that made me fall for him, he has a great heart, great personality and a great sense of family traditions, that is what I was looking for all along, and with those qualities, that made him so appealing to me".

MELISSA AND JOSHUA

Me: "so does an open marriage really work for you?".

Melissa: "For me yes, but it is not for everyone, the trust level must be there, and both must be really open for it, because if you are not open to it, it will most likely not work at all".

Me: "have you ever at any point in time in this open marriage relationship, felt jealousy?".

Melissa: "of course, I am a woman after all, but we have agreed on this and I know I can trust him, and I just try and not let it bug me, and if it does, then we just talk it out".

Me: "How do you manage to not let it bother you?".

Joshua: "I just do not think about it, I know what will probably happen but I just know that in the end she is coming home to me, and I am coming home to her, and we both love each other".

Me: "If you and Melissa were not in an open relationship, do you think that you would be together now?".

Joshua: "yes of course we would be together, this open relationship is not going to be around for ever, it is something just to spice things up a little".

Into Her Eyes

I look into her eyes
And I see nothing but beauty,
I am falling in love
With my heart really beating,

I want to take you to paradise
An island for you and me,
As we look at the sunset
With the soothing ocean breeze,

You are the one
The one that relieves my pain,
The one that I think of
When I am stuck in the rain,

You are the reason
The word love was said,
You make me feel alive
I am so glad we met,

I look forward to tomorrow
I look forward locking hands,
Having you in my life
Including you in my plans,

You are the one
The sunshine in my life,
I have fallen in love
As I look deep into her eyes.

SPECIAL THANKS!

I would like to take this opportunity to give thanks to, Tom and Jessica, Michelle and Steven, Jorge and Christina, Jose and Jennifer, Mike and Debra, Miguel and Stephanie, Melissa and Joshua, Justin and Megan, and a special Thanks to Peter and Susan, the pinnacle of true love. I would also like to thank all of my true friends who have supported me throughout all of my life, my family especially I love you all, and to my beautiful little girl and little boy, I love all of you dearly, and wish nothing but happiness for everyone.